I0453529

minutes in the arc

mary ellen weir

Copyright © 2023 by Mary Ellen Weir

All rights reserved.

Cover design by Julia Wohlers.

Composition by Linda Makarov.

Cover art courtesy of NASA.

Contents

Acknowledgments

To the various family members who appear in this book, who spoke to me so clearly, thank you for allowing me to interpret your story. Some of you I knew; some of you I only knew through hearing memories; some of you I had never heard of before. Thank you all for living within me.

To my mother Dorothea Joan Hennigan and my father William Franklin Weir...for words left unsaid to you both, thank you. And, the letter my father wrote to his mother Grace, announcing his engagement to my mother (found on pages 11-14) is the impetus for this book.

To my family and friends who have supported and encouraged by listening to the various stages of the book. Thanks to my brother, Charles, for being the first reader of a rough rough draft, and to my sister, Susan, for editing suggestions, and to both for adding to my own memories of who is who in the family. To my niece Kathryn Owens, who took time from her duties as managing editor of *The Foreign Service Journal* to edit and format the text. Her contribution made even more valuable as she, too, holds within her the people who speak in this book. My gratitude to Julia Wohlers, for her help in cover design, and Linda Makarov, for composition. Special thanks to the newly re-found Weir cousins, especially Pamela Weir-Quiton and Phyllis

Weir-Gladney, whose encouragement and help only enhanced the profundity of our re-connection. Thanks also to cousins George Weir Thompson, Tom Weir, and Beth Weir Tilson for their contributions as a family's re-connections enlarge.

To readers: thank you for reading. The intent of this book is to unfold, like an apple that is slowly peeled. I have not provided a family tree; I hope that as you read backward in time, the lives will piece together. That is my intent; if this is not clear by the book's conclusion, my apologies.

Introduction

The premise of this book is that life is always, that existence is eternal. Much like ancient Greek thought (most notably Plato's), similar ideas in Islam, Hinduism and other eastern religions, the assumption here is that we humans and our souls have a pre- and post-mortal existence. We were also created to have an empirical existence—our material, bodied, life on earth. We live out these lives, then our bodies die, and we return to our post-mortal existence. I call the earthly time of bodily life the "arc." Our lives on earth are our "minutes in the arc."

As William Wordsworth writes in his poem "Intimations of Immortality," we may come into our earthly existence "trailing clouds of glory" from our pre-mortal life, but we quite soon forget that existence as we grow and experience the realities of corporeal life. Thus, all we know is that our lives are "real" by virtue of our bodily presence. Our physical existence, then, becomes our everything. Consequently, is one of the strongest of human fears that of losing our embodied selves...that when our bodies are lost, our existence too will be lost?

Is this fear countered by the many and varied efforts we undertake to keep our stories and our ancestors' stories living and true?

Our ancestors' lives create our one individual life. Their passions, sorrows, achievements, inner unspoken thoughts, outer spoken thoughts, loves, sufferings, bad behaviors, good behaviors, aversions, delights, joys all somehow settle into each one of us, the who we are, paradoxically, as a singular person.

But as we know, our individual and ancestral stories are never just ours, belonging only to our family units. Those stories are just tiny sentences, not long at all, in the grand history of varied, complex, majestic, aesthetic, delicate moments of life on earth for cells, plants, animals, amphibians, and so much much more, both of discovered species, extinct species and species to come.

The human species is just one among all these. And in its evolution from the earliest bi-pedal hominids, *Australopithecus,* to *homo habilis*, and more advanced use of tools, to *homo erectis,* and migration, discovery and use of fire, to *homo neanderthalis,* and food economy and storage, to the current species of humans, *homo sapiens,* our nearest ancestor who developed culture and art.

And did they all...these ancestors who birthed and birthed over and over and over to bring us to us today, did they all and do we want to leave something of ourselves behind?

We do. I do. And hence this book.

Represented here are the lives of various persons, at various historical periods, in one extended family of humans: the paternal line of Weir, Watson, and Thomas, and the maternal line of McDonnell, Cox, and Hennigan. These names begin the telling backwards of various narratives. Some are memories I heard from childhood about the family, others the result of research, others are imaginary. Thus, you are reading a type of "biographical fiction." I try to speak their voices through my voice, which admittedly is impossible. I hope I represent all the people who appear in this book as honestly as they spoke to me.

Most importantly, and for some reason, they chose to first speak to me. I did not choose them; they chose me. And so I wrote what I heard from them.

To be biographically truthful to their lives, I have researched records, census documents and much more. However, I know some of the dates for their "minutes in the arc" may not be accurate.

I have tried my best to be true to them. I hope in that attempt I have served them well and, as St. Francis says, "have done what is mine to do."

minutes in the arc

if every earthly life

lives itself in an arc

an arc so seamless

with colors blending and so full of belief

in each life in its sweep,

lives that came from no beginning,

and go to no ending,

but there in the arc, having minutes

in finite time, earthly time,

a middle of certain minutes

given to each life in the arc.

When the minutes are up,

Look...there—

past its bend—there, where the arc swells to infinite,

to encircle yet again

the round stroking heavens

November 3, 2022

Sunday afternoon
May 16, 1948

Dear Mother:

This is rather momentous
news I have to tell you today.
I asked Dorothea to marry me
the last Thursday night and as a
result I am now engaged. You
know pretty well how I feel about
her; I have been with her practically
every day for almost a year. I know
she's the girl I want and am
prepared to accept the difference in
religious background.

We are going to be married
at the start of my vacation which
will be July 31. We have tentative

plans to spend about a week at one
of the lakes in northern Indiana
and of course to stop and see you
and the others. I hope to find an
apartment by that time and to spend
the second week fixing it up and
getting settled. We bought our first
cooking pot yesterday at Kroger's. It
was one of those pieces you get at a
reduced price when you buy so much
groceries. Dorothea asked if she could
buy it and started to pay for it,
but I thought I might as well get
used to it early so I told her to
keep the 2 dollars and — I paid for
it. She seems quite thrilled and I
really am too. Said she hasn't slept
hardly at all the last two nights.

Now don't start worrying about us,
Mom, and wonder if we'll get along
or have enough money to pay the
bills. I have thought everything over &
still realize that both of us will
have to learn & accept many things
as we go along, but after all thats
the way life is. Nothing comes easy, but
of all the girls I have ever known,
its Dorothea that I want to experience
~~of~~ life's problems with. I hope you
are happy for me and don't feel
like you are ~~or~~ losing a son; you
are just gaining a daughter. Don't feel
left out of things; I'll regard you
as my mother and her as my wife.
I love you both. Do you see
what I'm trying to say? you'll always

be one of my best girls.

I don't know when I will come up next. I'd like to bring Dorothea with me before we get married. Write and let me know when you will have the next week-end off.

Hope you won't be bowled over at this news, Mom, just realize that this won't change our relationship one bit.

Love,
Frank

William Franklin
Weir

minutes 1917-1988

June 20, 1933

There is a certain futility to writing a journal. I am the only reader. Yet I want a reader somewhere...who knows when and where, to understand me. My life. But the irony: I have to hide this journal and then destroy it...if my brothers ever found it and read it, I would be the laughingstock of Bloomington High School. I'd be deemed "Frankie with the diary," no doubt. Just like a girl, crying in her diary.

Well, I write for me. Maybe no one else ever will, except me.

I wrote this poem the other day; it makes sense to me.

I know that starry minds sigh their sighs

When, like housecats caged in windowsills,

They spend their lives seeing things beyond

December 10, 1933

Warren and Dad and I went to the site of the train accident. Picked up the bodies.

Oh. Can't even touch the experience. I should be used to it now.

I don't know how Dad and Mother do it. Of course, they know all the mortician tricks to make the bodies seem whole again.

April 17, 1940

I think I write poetry better than prose...like in these journals. The prose sounds so sophomoric, so mundane, no passion or stirring. I'll just write my poetry from now on.

It comes more naturally. I feel these phrases or words in my head. Not complete thoughts. Just a phrase that stirs me, that I know is tapping, tapping like a gentle knock at the real feeling or thought or image.

June 24, 1941

Went with Dad to register for the draft. I wanted to go to medical school, after college. Even though I failed Chemistry. Too many parties at the Sig Ep house got me on that one.

Started reading Thomas Wolfe's *Look Homeward, Angel.*

I feel I'm in the book. I'm Eugene Gant! Wolfe has created me, my family in the characters! I'm reading about the most inner me in the book. How does Thomas Wolfe know me, us, so well?

March 11, 1942

What do I do with all my poems? This journal? I've hid them away so no one can find them. They'd laugh at me, I think.

I wait to be drafted.

where does smoke come from?

I ask

my fraternity brothers—thinking they know me.

Sitting by the house fireplace, the fire jumping, at first, then trailing, then slightly smoking

wavy spirals that live, then vanish.

"Where does smoke come from? Where does it go to?" I muse.

They scoff: "from fire, you idiot!! You ask such obvious questions, Frank, don't you think before you ask such elementary questions? ... no wonder you're failing Chemistry!!" They all laugh...I meekly laugh, too.

I can't fight this.

But I know one thing: the deeper questions not visible in certitude's knowing.

With surety the chemical processes can be explained, and science holds its seeable truths.

But another truth mingles with that:

what grace lies just through the thisness of things,

what loving elegance hides past the folds of our numbed eyes, our bounded words...

while most cannot yet taste that different knowledge

some do see, dimly, the glorious chemistry of things.

(oh! it is a lonely life!)

November 2, 1938 / November 2, 2022

I want a poet

poet, write

the poem

that came in phrases

feelings ajar

when, numb at 14, I would help my father E.T.,

my brother Warren

collect in pieces shattered bodies from the railroad
tracks to place,

to make respectable in those caskets

of Weir Funeral Home.

write the poems

write for those moments entombed in me

May 3, 1933 / May 3, 2021

the idea of more, in two parts

I.   ***no more***

lying here

looking out at green

in the waking spaces each day.

each night.

the several conscious moments

looking out at green.

I 've seen enough of that.

I decided to go to bed

And never again rise

I decided not to eat

And never again be hungry.

Those curious and sophisticated years

Of only the best

Cigars, food, whiskey, books, Thomas Wolfe,

Music. Sometimes I still hear "Bolero" in my mind.

Peer Gynt "The Hall of the Mountain King,"

Segovia's guitar,

Sometimes I still feel the taste the smell,

Of sweet strong tobacco

In my pipe. I see the humidor full

Of my cigars, the *Bon Appetit* and *Gourmet* magazines,

Knowing the best foods, the best restaurants,

Joe's Stone Crab in Miami: the very best.

No more of that.

I'm tired.

What has tired me?

Was it all the disappointments? That still hollow pain—

My father leaving my mother. Rumors of other women, other children. I snapped at Carolyn: never never say that!

The war that kept me from medical school.

To console me, my brothers called me Doc.

The appendicitis that kept me from the Air Corps. The Air Corps that eagerly took my brother Charles,

Golden Charles. Warren my brother, the bright hope.

He would be mayor of Bloomington someday. It was part of the plan.

Just my little sister Carolyn and me, in the middle.

I knew Dorothea was the one. My mother was not happy

With my marrying a Catholic.

Unheard of.

But she came to the wedding.

Our children were joy for me. Always.

In later years, Dorothea said I projected onto them

my hopes for myself at their age,

All three so successful in careers, Susan became the doctor I didn't,

Chuck the lawyer, the soldier, Ellen the English professor.

II.   *more*

I feel a change in me

Like all is ending in me.

Is this the ending of me?

Dorothea comes in; kisses my forehead.

She says: "I love you, Frank."

I say a weak, unguarded pause between each word: "I love you very much."

I wonder if she really ever did love me.

Is she only saying it now, as I

Begin this ending?

She has brought in her rosary.

She says a "Hail Mary."

I never was a churchgoer. But I always tried to respect Dorothea's...or anyone's religion.

She raised the kids Catholic. I admired that.

I respected that.

Ellen became a nun.

I was proud of that.

Once, more was never enough.

Now, more is past.

The green outside is growing dim—

blurry—

—what?

"are you ready?"

—what?   what am I hearing?

something says Come, if you're ready.

The green is dissolving,

But nudges to the end...of an arc?

The bottom...of some kind of arc?

This sifting turns to luminous

I see luminous,

A radiant...a sphere?

—Oh I hear music ! roundness spheres

Like a—

Ah!

Why—

You are!

I am!

more.

June 24, 1988 / June 24, 2023

Fannie Amanda Watson minutes 1882-1920

What I saw

I can't describe.

all the time

there was no time

14 hours, 18 hours a day.

just keep going, tending, moving from one mat, one bed
to the other.

dress wounds, irrigate, cleanse with warm water

what was left

of a limb, a face, a hand.

if the wounds were not too bad,

let them heal. Then send the boy back to the front
again.

the gas casualties were the worst. So much unknown
in this

mustard gas. Poisonous gas.

the lungs would labor the coughing raw,

the vomiting,

the spitting blood.

clean up   wash.   Try to sooth.

sometimes we had to wear the gas masks ourselves,
to tend these forms,

these figures of humans,

whose faces, too, had to be masked.

we first both looked for each other's eyes

finding them small, beneath

the large unnerving manufactured eyes

big as frogs.

breathing in the air of the mask.

sometimes driving the ambulances, other times
assisting in surgery.

in the mobile unit, going so close to the battlefields,
we could hear the explosions, choke in the clogging air.

at the base hospital, mostly going bed to bed,

mat to mat, cleaning the dirt out of the wounds.

the germy dirt of the trenches.

the hardening of the mud

in the wounds.

only when I got sick—so many had the Spanish flu—

only when I got sick   too sick to serve,

and the contagion of the flu

was I discharged.

sent home on the transport with so many.

to think I had never been out of Indiana

and then traveled across and back a sea

I had only read about, could never image

in my land of cornfields and woods and hills.

what a wide sea! Sometimes friendly

other times quite unfriendly.

so many of the nurses were seasick.

I was too, and the bunks were hard.

only then, on the way back across the sea, did the images of what I saw

begin.

only then, in the hard rolling bunkbed, had I finally stopped

to see and feel the images, the memories

come rippling and harshing every nerve plume of every nerve tendril.

I was sick. In my body and my mind felt sick.

they talked about shell shock. To keep my head,

I faced I was shell-shocked.

I remember my older sister Grace

telling me stories of E. T.'s grandfather William

in the War Between the States.

how he did not talk of what he saw. How, on his return
from war

he was quieter. Just different.

and so I found some comfort in thinking I was not
alone.

I tried to slow the things I saw,

To face them head-on. Look straight in the eye

the going mat to mat, bed to bed, to each exploded
body

day after day after day in France.

I never had regrets joining

the Army Nurse Corps in 1917.

even though my health never regained itself

after getting home, trying to adjust.

I started sewing dresses, mending clothes.

that helped.

the focus on just one thing.

seeing just the needle and the cloth

and for a few blessed minutes,

not the other things.

my heart was sick.

my heart was sick.

and I died not believing that the

brutality I saw could be so

because of politics and power struggles and economics
and greed

that sent the faces, the eyes, the eloquent life of each
soldier I tended

to such ruin.

I died not believing that demolishing of life

could be so.

August 4, 1920 / August 4, 2023

Gilbert Thomas Weir
minutes 1855-1922

water carries everything

water carried everything

sleeked the soil

for the sun's greening

then, on our farm.

along with crops grew our children

the plants   the fruit   now gone

our children now gone

to think water carries everything

from its first moments on earth   then stirring all the way

through geologic time

all the way

to our farm in Indiana

and what seeds grown then

water still carries

January 5, 1922 / January 5, 2022

Nancy and Gilbert had children

After I died in 1922,

I kept close watch on our children.

One, Elijah Thomas, was your grandfather.

You only met him twice?

Your father Frank adored him;

Your mother said E. T. was a philanderer, a drinker.

He left your grandmother, Grace.

He left her with four children, she said.

Ran off with another woman. Everything collapsed after that. Their funeral home in

Bloomington. Everything collapsed.

Your aunt Carolyn said he had a second family, somewhere.

Your father was in England, during the war, when he received the letter.

Your father has left us.

He shattered that day.

You said you met E. T. twice?

First time, outside a one-room cabin, in the woods.

You tell me he seemed kind, meeting his four-year-old granddaughter for the first time.

His eyes drew you, you said.

The second time, a few years later, you were twelve?
Frank took you all to visit him,

living in a Quonset hut.

The grass had just been cut.

He had made a plate of tomato sandwiches, sliced into
nice squares, and aesthetically stacked.

No one ate them.

And to this day, you say you still feel sadness. He was

Kind, hospitable. But no one ate the sandwiches.

He looked at you again, kindly. A blink of softness, a
closed lip smile,

A look that you felt he wanted to last

On your face, your eyes.

Later that year, you were in the kitchen

The day your mother called Frank, far miles away.

To tell him my son, his father died.

She: direct, New England, but gentle.

You say what you could hear was silence

From far away.

A silence that thundered all the miles.

November 8, 2022

Rebecca Thomas Weir

minutes 1832-1911

unknown

to feel unknown

to be unknown

do we feel it first, and think that is our being?

are we destined to be what we feel?

do we choose?

I feel unknown.

only the words that walk so intimately

in my head that sculpt an inside

no one knows or sees

these words I do not know how to write.

Eliza is learning her letters

at school. She is teaching me the alphabet.

she is six and she loves showing me her tablet,

telling me the letters. We say the letters.

then we both try writing the letters.

I wish I had gone to school.

only the words in my head know me

and I know them.

I am unknown

but known: wife to William, mother to our children,
neighbor to our neighbors.

seen

and thoroughly unseen.

for who comes to me

day in day out

who comes to me in words as I wake to light

its first holy tiptoe

seems so very holy and the words begin and God begins
in all the words

and I am known

but oh! how do I ever tell of this

from my muteness?

I want a poet.

March 11, 1853 / March 11, 2022

can a shadow speed?

there seems to be light

driving through shadows. Streaking through shadows.

shadows of no color.

I saw all this, down where the train thundered by on the tracks. The train

so heavy so hard made shadows

through light.

I was holding Gilbert. He cried in the roar.

what is this thing? Speed.

what blares does it bring to our ears?

rough, contagious abuses of blares,

hurting both inner ears and outer ears.

new ears old ears.

speed in light and speed in shadows

does it all radiate us so, affect us so

that we so deeply cry?

speed   shadows   lights.

charts?

brought up out of us to map our way?

such an ache to know

is that why we cry?

September 12, 1856 / September 12, 2022

where did you go?

where did you go tonight

egg of the moon?

oval of the moon,

where have you gone tonight?

with the clouds

thrumming   so so slow

blurry bright

shady white humming

they call me William's wife.

I am really your wife, moon.

but wherever have you gone?

you alone who know my very blood

in your craters   your craters in my veins

but

where did you go tonight?

October 23, 1863 / October 23, 2021

the veil lifted

walking with Gilbert

in the familiar wood

just-born autumn is peeping in,

that summer smother lifting, a bit

all the leaves

splashed in light

with breathing,

everything is lifting, breathing

suddenly!

    —What?

the veil is lifted:

in just one single leaf,

the curtain opens in just one leaf, lower than the others

right before us,

looking in our eyes

One leaf alight

enflashed   enfleshed

look! Gilbert!   here's God!

                    September 10, 1860 / September 10, 2021

what Rebecca knows

Rebecca Thomas Weir saw a cockroach in the kitchen.

A very large roach. She saw it

moving

Up the wall sideway on the wall across the wall

Down the wall   explorer in a new land.

Antennas so long and reaching,

Feeling the surface roundness

Dullness bumps bruises

Of a human kitchen wall. Interacting.

Maybe like the moon, Rebecca muses as she watches,
maybe like the moon if humans ever go to the moon.

Explorers.

Like if humans ever went to the moon, interacting.

What a perfect body the roach has—legs with razors
along their reach to catch all kinds of surfaces   simple
complexity

What a wonder!

Large protective back-shield

What a wonder!

Rebecca reasons:

Yet I am large and powerful,

Compared to this

explorer in my kitchen.

Or intruder?

They say bugs bring danger, disease to us with their

Dirt, their ugliness.

They invade our houses

(like William fighting the Southern invaders. They shot at us first

at Fort Sumter.

William is killing invaders in the South now, away in war).

Rebecca thinks:

Oh, I know I do not know much. So many things I cannot know.

But I know this roach is a living wonder,

So shall I kill this living wonder

They say is our enemy?

Shall I kill this living wonder before it can kill me?

Our children? shall I murder this living wonder?

This holy?

No. I will not.

(and this is what Rebecca Thomas Weir knows)

February 4, 1862 / December 21, 2022

	Name	Place	Enlisted	Mustered	Remarks
	THOMAS GRIMES	Lewis	Aug. 15, 1862	Sept. 2, 1862	Promoted 1st Lieutenant.
	WILLIAM S. HUBBERT	Terre Haute	Sept. 4, 1862	Sept. 4, 1862	Promoted 1st Lieutenant.
	LAWRENCE BURGETT	Terre Haute	April 1, 1863	May 10, 1863	Mustered out with Regiment.
D	*Captain.*				
	WILLIAM REEDER	Rockville	Aug. 8, 1862	Sept. 2, 1862	Resigned June 10, '63.
	CALEB BALES	Toronto	Oct. 1, 1863	Nov. 5, 1863	Mustered out with Regiment.
	First Lieutenant.				
	DARWIN B. OTIS	Terre Haute	Aug. 8, 1862	Sept. 2, 1862	Mustered out with Regiment.
	Second Lieutenant.				
	CALEB BALES	Toronto	Aug. 8, 1862	Sept. 2, 1862	Promoted Captain.
	ELISHA PIERCE	Clinton	Feb. 15, 1864	April 11, 1864	Mustered out with Regiment.
E	*Captain.*				
	JEFFERSON E. BRANT	Terre Haute	Aug. 19, 1862	Sept. 2, 1862	Promoted Major.
	ORIN MCANDERSON	Terre Haute	Sept. 1, 1864	Oct. 30, 1864	Mustered out with Regiment.
	First Lieutenant.				
	ORIN MCANDERSON	Terre Haute	Aug. 19, 1862	Sept. 2, 1862	Promoted Captain.
	JOHN GUNN	Prairieton	Sept. 1, 1864	Jan. 28, 1865	Mustered out with Regiment.
	Second Lieutenant.				
	JOHN GUNN	Prairieton	Aug. 19, 1862	Sept. 2, 1862	Promoted 1st Lieutenant.
	MILTON W. HENDERSON	Prairieton	March 18, 1865	April 2, 1865	Mustered out with Regiment.
F	*Captain.*				
	WILLIAM D. WEIR	Prairie Creek	Aug. 15, 1862	Sept. 2, 1862	Resigned July 14, '64, for the good of the service.
	FRANCIS M. RUDE	Terre Haute	Oct. 1, 1864	Oct. 30, 1864	Mustered out with Regiment.
	First Lieutenant.				
	HIRAM L. TILLOTSON	Prairie Creek	Aug. 15, 1862	Sept. 2, 1862	Promoted Adjutant.
	FRANCIS M. RUDE	Terre Haute	Sept. 1, 1864		Promoted Captain.
	LEWIS W. WELLS	Terre Haute	Oct. 1, 1864	Nov. 1, 1864	Promoted Adjutant.
	JOHN W. BARLOW	Moscow	May 1, 1865		Mustered out as 1st Sergeant with Regiment.
	Second Lieutenant.				
	LAWRENCE W. HUTCHERSON	Prairie Creek	Aug. 15, 1862	Sept. 2, 1862	Resigned July 1, 1864; cause, disability.
	REUBEN CLARK	Prairie Creek	May 1, 1865		Mustered out as Sergeant with Regiment.
G	*Captain.*				
	ELLERY C. DAVIS	Terre Haute	Aug. 15, 1862	Sept. 2, 1862	Resigned July 20, 1864; cause, disability.
	FRANCIS C. CRAWFORD	Terre Haute	Sept. 1, 1864	Nov. 1, 1864	Mustered out with Regiment.

muster out roll, 85th Infantry Regiment, Indiana volunteers, Company F

William D. Weir under letter F

linger

I think about the word "linger."

it sounds itself, sweet in me, in my inner,

and I wonder at it.

I hear it sound my head. Maybe Eliza can show me how to read it,

write it.

write it on paper so that it sounds outside my inner,

births itself as a word: bodied, recognized, articulated in my outer.

I want to see how its letters look on a page.

I first sensed the word at the store in town.

I saw my neighbor Jane linger, touch with a linger

touch a bolt of cloth, linger

I saw her linger and just a moment stay, just a slight stay

in that one moment. I lingered watching her linger.

later I thought, what is it to linger?

why do we linger?

William lingered that day he rode to join his infantry troop.

his Captain's uniform so blue so clean

but he lingered as he waved goodbye. To stay, just a moment there to stay.

what is a linger? The moment of a linger?

oh these thoughts these words in me oh to give them bodies!

they linger. I want them to stay.

I want a poet.

May 3, 1862 / May 3, 2022

Both and beyond

what if there is both and beyond?

we seem to stay in "or,"

"this or that"

"sand or sky," "corn or wood"

what if there is both

and a beyond both?

what if there is a blending of both

male and female

in our child Thomas, and maybe a beyond both?

does he live in a place we cannot see now?

both and beyond?

before he left for war

William was so hard on Thomas—

chastising him for wanting to wear Eliza's dresses, her ribbons,

her frock

but then, playing like a boy with boys

on the schoolgrounds

and then again, playing dolls with the girls

on the schoolgrounds

oh Thomas! Have we named you an impossible name?

February 4, 1863 / February 4, 2023

William's letter to Rebecca

Stripped I am, my dear Rebecca:

In the South here is

soil so red like blood.

When I first saw it, I thought:

maybe the blood from all the battlefields

has so drenched the South

that its soil turned red.

A strange soil,

and withered rivers too.

Just cracks and dust and diminution

flakes and fractures and rust

where life once was.

Water, green essence.

And now Rebecca, I must tell you this:

I have been stripped

of these Captain's bars.

They said I must

"resign for the good of the service."

I don't belong here anymore.

They are sending me home.

They are banishing me.

I am the withered river

I am the strange red soil,

I am stripped to dust and rust.

I want back the brown black soil

I want back the green river

I want back my blood pumping rich life again.

I want a second coming.

July 24, 1864 / July 24, 2021

Rebecca's poem to William

Eliza, poor child, read me your letter.

I of sudden feel capacities, William.

distance makes it easier sometimes

to openly speak the truth.

William: captain.   coward?

what led you to it? This "it" so vague and muddy.

"resigned for the good of the service."

what does that mean?

did you have a choice? were you a coward?

were you drinking? were you wrongly accused?

what about us? what about me?

was there someone else? was there something else?

you never knew me. you only called my name as: "William's wife."

us: joined (but not).

if we meet in an afterlife, will we tell each other the truth?

or like here, will we choose again to stay lost, walking vague dusky forests?

August 6, 1864 / August 6, 2021

have I?

have I taken love?

I've given it, I know.

but have I taken it?

is love just given to fields ablaze,

crazed with too much sun

or wet with rain and creamy light?

I have given this love, working fields, raising children.

but have I taken love

without inner objection, remonstrance,

doubt?   Love just given to me

without logic or explanation?

I don't think I have taken love much.

having gone through courtship with William,

marriage, children. His shame which became our
shame.

now, in this night

so dark

with the day's great tangle finally still,

the fields come clearer than ever

do I at last seem to see?

the fear has always been me.

September 15, 1867 / September 15, 2022

I think it takes a lot

I.

I think it takes a lot

to be born

to know it's time to be born.

but not knowing what

that push is—

not understanding what that push is—

some kind of tugging, pushing

prodding to leave the dark warm.

leaving.

leaving warm—

oh!   Oh!

　　—what?

and then you look amazed!

and then you see

the lovely place.

II.

I think it takes a lot

to die

to know it's time

to die.

but not knowing what that push is—

Not understanding that coming tugging pulling

push

(like what it would be like to jump from the sky

that first time

being pushed right out of the sky just when the fear
clenches   most clenches)

    oh!   Oh!

     —what?

and then you look amazed!

and then you see

the lovely place.

December 18, 1887 / December 18, 2021

beating giant

what if we could hear

earth's heart?

do we hazily hear it, here in our feet,

through our feet, walking this giant heart?

do the galloping long run horses dimly feel the

beat, too? And run run run faster faster to hear that
lavish music?

what if we felt the giant blood streaming

in our own dwarf hearts,

rivers and rivers of stream sparkling beauty of

the giant heart

to hear what is here...right hear

October 25, 1888 / October 25, 2021

arc?

so this is who I am and

who I am born to and

how I grow up and the time I live and

who I marry and

the children I birth and

how I die

and all this is life...

why...it seems like an arc?

May 23, 1911 / May 23, 2022

The book of beginning

is that how you started it?

mixing the blue storm:

those things they call atoms, magnetism,

the fire, the gusts

feeling it all in your blood

the blasts of forces and fire

knowing, feeling, seeing the congealing

building, building, bellowing

to a never-ending expansion.

One night

William read to us all, in front of the fire.

Chapter One of The Book of Genesis

The book of beginning.

How you created the earth in six days. And then tired,

You rested.

With you resting, the children became tired, too.

And William.

I put the children to bed; William curled in our bed.

All tired. I was tired, too.

But I stayed alone by the fire, thinking of fire.

mending the socks, the shirts.

And I wondered: the wonder of how you started it all, us.

Who you are.

And now, long dead on the earth

But so very alive here, I watch

The scientists, the chemists, the astrophysicists in
their labs

Writing their papers. Now I watch

How the history of thought and science has progressed
since that night by the fire.

Amino acids protons quarks theories of everything

Molecules microbes

Shaking cajoling rumbling

To birth   birth   birth

So much beyond what we could ever imagine

That night by the fire,

With William

reading from the Book of Beginning

January 30, 2023

Dorothea Joan Hennigan

minutes 1924-2013

Dorothea

Mommy, why did Jumbo kill the bird?

—Jumbo is just being a cat.

No! Jumbo is bad! Why was Jumbo bad?

—Honey, God makes cats to be cats

And that's how cats get their food.

But we feed Jumbo. Jumbo rides in my doll carriage.

June 20, 1929 / June 20, 2022

October 18, 1938

Dear Gloria:

I have to explain what I meant on the bus the other day.
I can't call you...my parents would hear. So I'm writing.
You can't tell ANYONE about Haig. If you do I will
never forgive you!! Never!!

Especially not Bill. You know the crush he has on me.
I like him. He's swell. He's nice. But.

I know it's hard to understand since you don't know
Haig and what it's like being in class with him at
Classical. Seeing him in the hallways. I just wish you
and I were in the same school!! Then you'd understand,
maybe?

After you get this—I slipped it in your mailbox—oh I
hope your brother doesn't see it!!—can we talk again on
the bus? You can tell Frances. But no one else!!!

Dorothea

March 9, 1945

Dear Gloria:

Oh...with graduation so close...it's scary. Now what happens in my life? No more school. I loved college; I really don't want to leave. Just learning so much...the professors, the books, the discussions. I know you never liked school that much, but even though we are so different, we truly understand each other.

I really would like to be a journalist. That's why I majored in English. I love words. Stories told. I love fiction. Never really liked poetry, though. Poetry just seems too vague, too illusory, too indirect.

I like to figure things out, put things together methodically, patiently, squarely so they all fit neatly together. That's why I minored in Math. Math is so clean. Something somehow is always going to equal something else. And it all works out evenly. Oh, I'm rambling. I will just miss college.

Maybe I'll apply for jobs at the *Providence Journal*. I'll probably end up working there for years and years... probably as a secretary, that's about as high as a woman can get in journalism. Or any area.

Oh. Gloria, I just want more than living the rest of my life in Rhode Island, being a policeman's wife. Bill will go into the Police Academy then on to the Department. My father already has made connections for him. You know how swell Bill is. He's kind and he's fun. You know I like him a lot. My parents love him; my dad especially. They really want me to marry him. We were all worried when he had to interrupt college to go off to the war. Thank God it's winding down, at least in Europe. Gloria: I'm thinking of breaking the engagement with Bill.

I know. Everyone will wonder why. Try to talk me out of it. It will hurt Bill so. You know how he loves me. I'm everything to him. Oh, this has me all roiled up inside.

I told grandma about it. I told her about Haig. She said she would never tell anyone. Just like you said you never would. And you never did. That means so much to me. Best friends. You and I. Frances, too.

I hope you understand. Somehow, I know you will. I just want more.

Dorothea

July 14, 1988

Dear Telia:

I appreciated so much your kind note of condolence.
I knew Frank's death was coming...I could just tell;
somehow we just see it in the face. But when it came,
it felt like my whole body came into my throat, and
I couldn't say words at all. 40 years together. I drove
home, alone, from the emergency room that night. Not
thinking, not feeling. Just a numb crush of everything.

Remember the day I told you Frank and I were engaged?
You and Cliff had just become engaged, too! Everyone at
the Manor was getting engaged. Sort of the thing to do!
The Manor at Seagrams...all us single female employees
housed...just like a dorm. Everyone talking about who's
dating whom and who got jilted and who's looking...oh
it was fun and high drama all rolled together. We "girls"
were just expected to marry and so we played out those
expectations.

I'm sorry it's taken me more than a month to write.
Taking care of everything, the funeral, all the
bureaucratic paperwork to be filed when a marriage
ends with death.

Just lately, after somewhat finishing up all the things
to be done, I finally felt such an enormous sadness.
Bleakness. One day, I was going through Frank's clothes,
when the doorbell rang. A delivery of flowers...from
an old boyfriend in Rhode Island! Bill. He had heard

through Gloria about Frank's death, the note said. Just wanted to send me flowers.

Oh: the flowers brightened my gloom. Oh. I just remember things lifting; a feeling of life coming back a bit.

I'll write more later. Hope Cliff is recovering. Thank you so much again for your kind sympathy note.

Dorothea

May 23, 1989

Dear Telia:

Today I'm marrying Bill. My gosh, who would have ever imagined? Being engaged 45 some years ago. I broke it off. Went to Indiana, met you and all our friends at the Manor, met Frank, married to him for 40 years with 3 children.

You and Gloria in Rhode Island got all those letters with me worrying about what would people think... the family...my children...what would they think about re-marrying a year after Frank's death? But Bill was insistent. He was so afraid I'd say no. Susan, Chuck, Ellen have been great about it. Bill's children are fine with it, too. They lost their mother 6 years ago.

As I told you, Bill and I will live winters at my house in Florida, summers at his beach house in Matunuck. Everything is just working out. Things always do.

Wish you could come to the wedding. Holy Sacrament Church in Providence. I feel like I'm coming home again.

Got to go but wanted to jot you this short note on my (second) wedding day!!

Dorothea

October 15, 2002
Dear Gloria:

Yes, you and Bob, Bill and me...we enjoyed such good times together those years I was back in Rhode Island.

I am adjusting to widowhood (again). It's taken these 3 years since Bill's death to re-establish myself to me. And to live alone, really, for the first time in my life. I do like the solitude, I must admit. And, just doing what I want when I want. That's nice. I have good neighbors here in Florida...so that helps, too.

The lovely home Frank and I built in the '70s was so nice with all the woods, the beach right across the street. But, sadly, like everywhere, the developers have come. All the lovely, jungle-woods are being destroyed for new homes, new condos, new beach resorts. Oh, it breaks my heart. I must tell you of this searing moment: I just happened to look out the window into the backyard...and what did I see but a Florida panther! At first I was startled. It was so big. But so slowly treading through the yard, not with power or command, but looking wary, uncertain.

Oh! I thought: I've thought it so many times: where do the animals go? Where do they go when their habitats are so cruelly...thoughtlessly...violently torn away. Oh, that sight broke my heart.

Write when you can. Say hello to Bob.

March 8, 2013

Dear Jean:

I included a short note in my Christmas card—thank you for yours!—but wanted to write more later. So here is later!

So nice to have you in North Carolina...although several hours away. I'm getting used to my house here. It's not home, though. I think you said you felt that, too, about moving to be closer to Margaret. Georgia was your home. Rhode Island was my home. But to think of how we met in Jonesboro, Georgia, both teaching English at the high school! What fun we had with the others in the teachers' lounge. What good times we had.

Now, I'm in a wheelchair. I spend my days at the dining room table, in front of a nice large set of windows. I read my books and I watch the birds. I wait for Ellen to come each day, and tell me all the happenings at the college, especially about the troublesome academic dean. The nerve of that woman! Reminds me of...oh, what was his name...the assistant principal we all couldn't stand. Oh...what was his name? Power hungry. If he only knew what we said about him in the teachers' lounge!

I wait for the caregiver to come.

Oh, what a way we all come in life. To old age. A sort of helplessness. You feel it, too, I know.

And things get smaller, simpler. Which is soothing, at least for me. I enjoy watching the birds at the feeder outside the window. Then in and through the bushes farther out in the yard. Sometimes there is great scattering when the squirrels come, trying to get to the feeder. The crows don't take too much of that. Nor the blue jays. Sometimes I see the neighbor's cat come sculking across the yard. I think of my cat Jumbo, when I was a little girl. I think the birds prefer the squirrel visits!

Oh...my hand is so shaky...I hope you can read this old lady scrawl.

I look forward to your next letter. Til then I'll watch the birds!

Dorothea

Catherine
McDonnell Cox

minutes 1875-1944

Catherine

It's 1943, wartime,

and I'm living on Union Avenue in Providence, Rhode Island

with my only living child Anna Cox Hennigan, her husband Charles,

and their only daughter Dorothea,

who is in her second year

at Pembroke, the women's college of Brown University.

Anna owns a dress shop, Charlie is a police officer,

and I stay here at home,

watching all the younger McDonnell cousins

who come over from Wood Street.

This is who I am now and how I live.

I am sixty-four years old,

and I think I may die soon.

So, you think it's time to talk about my life and story?

I don't know you, though.

You tell me you are my yet unborn great granddaughter.

You tell me you are the youngest child of Dorothea Hennigan and William Franklin Weir who will marry in Indiana in 1948!!

Why so far away? Indiana??

And he a Protestant!! Not a good idea!

New England Catholics should not marry Indiana
Protestants.

I'm not happy about my granddaughter marrying this
person,

but Charlie and Anna are OK with it so I keep quiet.

I don't understand this.

This telling me the future

While you want me

To talk about my past.

You seem odd to me.

*

So...is it Ellen or Mary Ellen, you go by?

At least they put some reminder of the Blessed Virgin
Mary

in your name.

My oldest sister's name was Ellen.

Maybe you are named after her?

You were born in 1953, nine years after I die?

You tell me

somehow you feel I've spoken to you, and you want

to have a conversation with me,

and other ancestors. Those you say speak to you.

That seems just far-fetched to me.

And why? Why do you think

You can possibly speak about our lives?

And how can your voice

Speak in our voice

About our lives?

We're all long gone.

It seems a bit silly to me.

And maybe I or others of them

don't want you speaking for us.

People tell me I'm brash. Hard.

Saucy. Too straight-talking...

But then you tell me maybe, somehow,

in some mysterious, sacred way,

the blood and soul connections of all these "us"

may merge in your blood and soul...

to write a story of human life and the historical times of these lives,

and the experience of one family's human journey.

A mirror of all the journeys

Of life on this earth.

Well.

I just know about mine.

Your title is confusing...*Minutes in the Arc.*

What's that mean?

First I thought of "ark." Noah.

But you say "arc" and then explain it.

I'm not too interested in that sort of thing.

But you asked for my story.

I decided to tell it

When you said

You found your mother's handwritten efforts

to sketch out the McDonnell and Cox family tree.

And all the pictures of us Anna had kept, then Dorothea had kept

In the old old album.

I remember that album. My mother Maria had bought it.

Excited by photography,

Hearing about all the families having portraits made.

She wanted that.

For someone to remember that we once

Had life.

That says to me Dorothea, like Anna, like Maria,

Wanted something preserved.

Something of us all to be remembered,

To be marked.

I guess this is your way of trying

To do the same thing they did.

*

I'm a McDonnell; my mother Maria

a Diffley.

All from County Roscommon, in Ireland, of course.

Why does life

Go by so fast?

As I get older, I go back more, in my mind.

I can see things,

So clearly,

Like it all just happened yesterday.

The images are so clear. I can almost

Touch them. Put them in

Front of me, live them again.

Oh I see it now: 1885

Leaving Ireland. I was 10. My sisters

Ellen, Mary, my mum, my da. Ellen only 11;

Mary 7.

I remember some parts of our leaving,

Like I am there, then,

And telling you right as I'm living those moments,

Right there in the moments.

Other things I don't remember the details as well.

And, maybe I'm filling in, now, as an adult, what my mum and da told me.

It all gets mixed, I guess,

in memories.

I remember we seemed to

Have traveled so far to get to Liverpool.

While I can see a bit the train ride from Roscommon to Derry,

I don't remember much of that,

Only just feeling astonished

At a new world I saw

More the feeling rather than

The sights.

On that second part of the trip,

On the ship from Derry to Liverpool. Just crowded.

Little Mary crying and fussy, I do

Think I recall that.

I don't remember too much

Only the feeling of being crowded.

It felt so harsh.

But the Liverpool dock I remember

keenly.

I see it like a picture

And I'm there. I'm there!

oh how I touch it now!

touch it. See it.

Just motion, motion on the dock.

Walking   walking.

My mum holding Ellen's hand, Ellen holding my hand

Me holding Mary's hand.

And da looking back always looking back to make sure we

Stayed together.

So many people

to steer through.

My father with the luggage,

Looking back, checking.

Our clothes in two sacks and the third sack

With the beddings, the cookware

The fourth sack empty now, to hold the food we would get

when we boarded the ship.

I remember my mum saying later,

The food was provided for us, included in the ticket price.

Salted meat. Ship's biscuits, flour, oatmeal porridge.

We would have to cook our own food.

So much fast motion. Hurry.   Hurry.

Then: we came to the big big biggest ship I'd ever seen.

So many people queuing before the giant.

This huge thing. I'd never seen such a towering thing

I was scared and excited all at once.

I had never seen such a big thing before.

My mum, my da, us all

Looking at that hulk, that enormous thing we would climb onto.

scared and excited. Mary with

her wide eyes

looking at the enormous thing.

My da later said

Our decision to leave Ireland had to come.

No work there. Still suffering from the potato famine.

There was no future for the Irish in Ireland.

My grandda Joseph

A tenant at the encumbered estate,

He couldn't pay the rent.

Ireland, all of Ireland: a pauper nation.

Joseph forced to the workhouse. The poorhouse.

A pauper of pauper Ireland.

My da Patrick born in the poorhouse, 1851.

It seemed all of Ireland had to get out.

It seemed they were all here on this dock.

Cramming the big ships for America.

But that was a comfort in the numbers leaving. That
soothed the fear feelings

A bit, with so many others like us.

Stepping onto this one big ship.

On that big sea. We were all together in

not knowing

What faced us

When we stepped off the giant ship

In America.

We were in steerage.

With so many more. Such a swarm of us...mostly all Irish.

So dark there. Damp, foul-smelling. Oh! the smells

I remember hearing the stories of why they left.

Who had paid everything they had, just like us,

For someone who had work to meet us

at the dock in New York,

who would help us find

a place to stay, help find work.

The smells, constant sounds. The smells,

Of the toilet, dirty clothes, dirty bodies. No air.
Just foul air.

All our clothes with the food smell.

It blocks you like a dirty puddle

Comes rising up from your clothes to your nose to your hair to your eyes

Then outward to all else.

That smell never went away. A week and a half of that

smell, those smells,

That damp. Dark. So often

The roll, the shudder of the big ship.

My mum would pray the rosary. She kept it in her pocket.

It seemed the only clean thing around.

And her prayer book. The women

And their prayer books.

Pages worn with the fingers touching

Touching the pages.

I use my mum's prayer book, her rosary

To this day.

I will pass them on to Anna.

Cockroaches and bugs. We had bunks   stacks of bunks.

With all dirty people

With our dirty smells.

Children playing.

Telling stories of Ireland. What some had heard about America.

The talk about

The "No Irish Need Apply Here" signs

On business fronts, storefronts

In the cities.

Where we would go.

Much coughing. Children crying. Then children sleeping.

We were only allowed to go on the main deck

The part where the most violent swaying

Of the ship seemed to be.

But just to get fresh air.

Over there, beyond the barrier,

We could see the first- and second-class

Passengers strolling,

Enjoying the air.

For us, we were on our deck to survive in that air.

Gasping in it,

Clutching in it.

And then, the cooking.

oh! I remember my mum telling about it.

It seemed every time, years later, when we were in our kitchen

On Wood Street, she would talk

Of the cooking on the ship.

We were assigned group times to cook our food.

In that tiny kitchen, with six other mothers, trying to fix a meal: salted meat, or the porridge, or the pea soup.

With the ship rolling, oh! It was so hard to cook, and the other

Six, trying to cook.

And that smell, cooking in our clothes.

And the day we first saw America!

News of seeing land spread through steerage.

Tiny land way way off. But the land!

Of course when word spread

And all took to pushing and shoving

To get up to deck to see.

Someone commanding "Order!"—

and so we took turns going up to see the land.

I remember with my da,

Him helping me up the stairs.

Tiny then less tiny less far off

the land grew.

Grew, grew bigger. Bigger.

Can it be so?

There is America. Can it be so?

Back in Ireland, the imaginings of America

In our minds. Our fantasy of America

Now there! Seeable.

Is it so?

The going on going on   closer, closer the land sprouted.

Then! We saw the city! We saw the city towers coming, coming!

Oh.

Joy.   Joy.   Not believable!

But here it is!

Here.

We saw then the island. We anchored right off the island.

We saw Castle Garden.

We stopped. The big big ship finally stopped.

Finally rested.

Back down now, be orderly

Gather the luggage and sacks.

One of the women put on her best hat.

"Want to look me finest for coming to America,"

she said. And she did look lovely.

Then back up the stairs pulling, grappling luggage and sacks

Helping the one ahead push up the luggage and sacks.

It took very long.

So many of us.

I remember my mum telling of the waiting

For the Inspector of Customs to board and examine luggage.

So much of it! Trunks, suitcases, but most with

sack bags.

After that,

It took so long and voices and movement,

Then Medical Officers came.

To inspect us: long lines to wait. Report any

Coughs or fever.

I looked at the island, the city beyond.

Oh the towers! It was April,

And the air smelled so fresh...

After that, the tugboats and barges came to transport us to the dock,

Where we would step onto America.

Almost there, we began to see

The idea of America

Moving on the dock. Dockworkers, horses, carriages, wagons,

All motion

And shouts and all

Seemed intent on their job. Everything seemed

Like a big gear.

All moving.

And again, off over there, the big buildings and towers.

the April fresh air.

huge ropes and shouts in docking the barges, the tugboat.

Now the big ship, out aways, could finally rest. Stop moving.

But not us.

We queue to go

to the big building. Castle Garden.

Long lines to get off the boat. Adults looking out;

I remember being squeezed going down the gangplank, and the movement stopping when

A little boy tripped, ahead of us.

But for once, a quiet in that slow passage down the
gangplank.

I thought that odd

Finally slow and quiet, after all the noise and voices of
the ship

But that slow movement down,

that unusual hush,

Offering us just an instant, just a flit of time

to realize in quiet,

the stepping onto America.

Then right off the gangplank, on the dock,

The noise and hurry again.

All directed

to the Castle Garden Rotunda

(that room so tall,

so upward looking). Oh it was wondrous

looking up

way way up there to the dome,

an inside sky!

then more and more long lines,

long tables with letters

To G-M we went.

Long tables with people in uniforms. Papers, stamps.

We stood in M. So long at M.

The man was very official.

He talked that odd American flat

and it was hard to hear,

with all the commotion.

Mum said it was hard to understand some of his words.

And even the words we could understand,

we didn't know what they meant in immigration talk or American talk.

My mum was tired, she said, and overwhelmed.

She asked the man to slow down,

to repeat what he said. He became impatient, as I suspect this was a

request he heard day after day after day

with every single person coming to the M table.

He snarled a bit: "Better learn fast.

This ain't Ireland no more."

Sting. Mum told us later how that stung

One of those times when someone's words slap so hard.

First stuns; then hurts so deep. Confuses.

And stays for a lifetime.

We were powerless and at his mercy, she said.

For an instant, the feeling of Ireland again.

But NO! we were in America.

He just pointed where to sign.

I can see now, like it's happening right now,

And I am there right now,

the wedding ring

on his hand.

Finally, to the Registry Department.

Names, intended destination.

After that, to the Railroad Ticket Office.

We didn't go there, as my mum and da had arranged to be met by

someone who would give us a place to stay,

help us find work. We had to wire the money, almost all

our money.

So we went to the Information Office. An officer called out names

of those having someone—

friends, relatives, who were waiting for them.

I felt safer here.

Just wait to be picked up

by this man my parents had paid.

My da said, when we get cleared and hear our name called,

we go outside

and look for a man with a sign with the name,

Patrick Joseph McDonnell.

Many Patrick or Joseph McDonnells were called.

We didn't know which one was my da's name.

We went when we heard Patrick Joseph McDonnell,

The three names in one, and got another paper stamped.

Then outside. Mary jumping up and down

seeing the horses, the wagons.

There were so many signs with the names, the wagons.

The patient horses.

People greeting their relatives sometimes. Others loading their bags

in wagons.

We looked and looked for our Patrick Joseph McDonnell sign, our wagon.

"Catherine, watch your sisters, stay right here don't move one inch

Maria go over there to look, I go the other, we'll keep looking.

Maybe way down there he is."

I ordered us not to move. Not one inch.

Mary still gleeful, pulling to see horses.

NO! we were both harsh with her.

We waited.

What happened? We paid for it! Where was that man with our name on the sign?

Oh I remember the fear. The drop in my body. Panic.

My da and mum eventually came back.

Trying to stay calm. But I saw their eyes.

Almost everyone had been met. Had ridden off.

Where was the man? Where was the wagon?

Da and mum how I think now of the panic they must have felt.

The whole stomach pit rising up. Choking the throat.

But they didn't show it. I think I learned

in that moment

not to show it.

What now? Where do we go?

Feeling like Ireland again.

Oh.

We didn't know what to do. Then a man with a wagon saw us.

Who is to pick you up?

We told him the man did not come.

This man said: do you want to go to

Rhode Island? To Providence. I can get you jobs there.

Well...what do we do?

Not trust the man? Trust the man? Are there choices?

Yes, always a choice. Always a hope.

But where?

My da and my mum made the choice.

Yes; take us to Providence, Rhode Island.

*

Oh what a sorrow losing Sedona was.

She was so pure and tiny. Eighteen months old.

She died a hot day, a bleak day,

a day with hot blaring sun

but no light at all.

September 13, 1902.

That day I don't want to see again. To feel again.

Blocked the day.

Oh. She was so sick. Poor suffering thing.

She cried and cried and took no comfort.

The crying just got weaker and weaker.

We didn't know what to do. The doctor came;

she was so sick. So violent was she sick.

We were so scared.

We kept her pink little booties.

Seven years later, Daniel died.

He was so young! My Daniel.

The alert eyes. Interested in everything.

And the wavy Irish hair.

Everyone loved Daniel. Loved him on

his route. The horse, the cart come bearing the supplies from O'Connor Bros.

So many customers came to the wake at the house

on Huntington Avenue.

The service at St. Mary's, from where we buried Sedona,

full of his friends and customers. My da loved Daniel.

He got Daniel the job of conveying supplies for O'Connor's.

O'Connor's rented the carts from my da's teaming business.

And then six years after that, in 1913,

my da was killed by the train.

My mum won't talk much of that day, either.

Just shut it away.

he had gone out at twilight

coming up, slowly gathering at 4:00 because of December,

gone to get

bread.

She needed bread for the pudding.

He went.

Had to cross the tracks...oh I can't talk of it.

It was all in the papers.

"Man killed by train."

"Owner of teaming business killed by train."

I shut the sorrow away. Mum shut the sorrow away.

God: where were you?

Far away.

do you even care?

You don't care.

You take so many from me.

All sudden taking.

How could you?

And yes! I dare speak to the Lord that way!

The Lord wants us to say what we think to Him.

But still I have my rosary.

My prayer book.

My mum Maria died in 1921.

Again they go.

Too much.

And I have already said too much.

Don't want to say it all.

My mum said my heart went steel on me

when Sedona died.

Then Daniel dying steeled me more, she said.

With each taking more and more sorrow

all poured and cemented in me,

this container of heartache.

that's the way I live.

But we had Anna in 1904.

Oh! Joyed a bit.

A sweet, lovely quiet baby.

A sweet, lovely woman now,

and marrying Charlie so good.

But with Anna as a baby,

Daniel and I always scared in the back of our heads

...not again.

Every time Anna would have a crying fit or get sick,

Daniel and I didn't talk...

we just soothed her, and we just kept going.

Do all that we must

and keep going.

We're Irish. We're Catholic. We just keep going.

They say I was always hard.

In Ireland they called me sharp-tongued,

A bit brash. Kept much inside to myself.

Could laugh and have great fun, but still:

"Catherine is so aloof."

I just don't think it's anybody's business.

But here I am, talking

like a bird chattering in the morning.

Maybe because I don't really think

you thinking

that you can speak our voices

says really anything.

Who says it's such great account?

But you saying something like it's the Communion of Saints

makes me wonder

if you still have Catholic in you.

For the sake of that, if it's so,

I'll keep telling.

my mum Maria died in 1921.

She was old, not like Sedona and Daniel. She just got old,

and it was her time to go.

But no matter the time, a mum's death

flattens.

Not like the suddenness and out of timeness as Daniel and Sedona and my da,

but losing your mother.

No words for losing your mother.

Charlie and Anna had only one child, Dorothea.

and I must say she whittled off a bit

that steel...but even when I found

myself giving my heart to her, my grandchild,

always, always was that fear that she, too

could be taken.

Do they never stop? The deaths.

But with Dorothea coming in April, 1924,

I felt my heart find some freshness again. Same as when

Anna was born, after Sedona.

Dorothea, such a smart child.

Curious, taking such delight in birds, our cat Jumbo,
flowers.

Ever everything a wonder to her,

Even as she grew; even in the high school years, now the
college years,

everything a wonder.

She was an only child,

but never alone for playmates

with all the McDonnell cousins

always in and out of the house.

The Union Avenue house always full of children.

In, out, running in the back yard. Jumbo running with them.

My heart found breezes again.

They all called her Dottie. Or Dot.

To think how everyone called her that name

and she took it well but never liked it.

Said she's no dot. She's no polka dot, she'd say.

I tried to call her as she liked.

And she wasn't a plain old Dot.

She was such a smart girl. Unusual for a girl.

Loved books and drawing and reading. And playing.

Loved Jumbo. And the neighbor's dog Alice.

the birds and chipmucks in the backyard.

Always loved the animals.

And so smart.

Selected to go to Classical High School. For the smart children.

She loved it.

Had so many friends. Had some boyfriends. But said it

Was really Haig. Always Haig, Haig this, that.

She had friends

who didn't go to Classical.

Gloria, Frances. Her very best friends.

Oh, they had fun times.

Oh...just remembered this.

way before, when Dorothea was just starting first grade, I

remember how Anna would walk her

the first couple weeks

to Wood Street School.

Only to be shocked when Dorothea turned up back at home.

She ran away from school. Fled right back home.

How she got out, we still don't know.

Got in trouble but kept running from school.

Why we thought when she loves learning and books?

What is it keeps her running from school?

Then one day, seeing the police officer helping with crossing,

he knew Charlie well,

Anna goes up to him with Dorothea in firm hand, said: officer.

My daughter here keeps running away from school.

What can you do about that?

He said: well, we'll have to arrest her and

put her in jail for a good long time.

Dorothea ran away from school no more after that.

We had a good laugh about it,

and Charlie said at the precinct the boys had a good laugh about it.

Congratulating themselves on effective police work!!

Then the time Jumbo killed the bird,

and she was so upset.

She asked her mother why Jumbo killed the bird.

Anna came in to tell me all about it.

Dorothea crying and crying

wailing why did Jumbo kill the bird?

Anna didn't know how to explain to a little bewildered betrayed four-year-old.

No one does.

Even as a child, your mother was very sensitive.

But as I watched her grow up,

I saw her more and more

live inside with her feelings.

Maybe it's what the McDonnells do.

She began learning to endure.

Just like me, I thought. Like her mother Anna.

Endure sorrow. Keep moving.

I think what is true endures.

You tell me you were with them

when they both died.

Anna. You were there.

Anna just dropped down and died. You were there.

You tell me you took care of Dorothea

in her final years. She wanted to stay in her home.

Never go to a nursing home. Just like Anna always said.

You tell me all this.

Hard years. But she stayed in her home.

She endured. Read her books every day.

She read so many books.

Watched the birds in her backyard.

Loved her cat.

With so much grace and dignity.

With steel she endured those years.

You tell me this.

You were with her when she died, you say.

Emergency room.

The surgeon had just told her

her aneurism would burst. Very soon. No surgery,
she said.

She knew. "It's time," she said.

"I'm ready. I'm not afraid."

She said you and your brother and sister made her
life so

wonderful.

Then, she gasped suddenly.

More gasps, then she died.

You tell me this.

Oh.

January 21, 1943 / January 21, 2023

Daniel Joseph Cox
minutes 1871-1909

what holds us up

it's easy to forget what holds us up

a chair, wood beam, floor, plank

the wagon I drive, the horse that pulls.

Catherine my wife, Anna our child,

Sedona, our dead child,

flower, field

air, earth, the blood sun today.

what holds us up? From where?

our bone, our mind

the stray cat on Wood Street,

the sailing clouds

the snow, rosewashing the blue

November 8, 1902 / November 8, 2022

air

accident.

are these my last moments,

so quickly come? abruptly

no warning.

just here. accident.

I lie in the road now.

how could this be?

they gather, shocked, wide-eyed.

my horse, my wagon. Horse panicked. Wagon tipped,

supplies to deliver spattered across this brutal road.

air   ways.

ways   of air.

the ways of air

that feed our red rich silt

that fertilize that red wine blood

for this river inside

that needs it so

air   ways   oh   air is going out of me

how I want back my face

a bit cheeky and pink.

April 25, 1909 / April 25, 2021

leaving the arc

is death a slow

going back to our womb,

when our body birthed in the arc?

and when our minutes in the arc

are over, do our bodies contract

to fill the womb

so that we can better begin

curling to that kindly warm, preparing us

to travel

way there, to the birth opening.

and as we grow smaller and smaller, we connect more

with that something up there in that bright

and we realize we can only live on with that light.

when we're ready, when it's time, when we know it's
time,

we feel the magnet drawing, drawing

towards the lightful opening,

and we curl to the beckoning

we small our bodies, to help the moving

and then slowly   slowly

they drop away,

our bodies,

and we finally see

the soul we could never see,

and this soul becomes our fullness, opening   opening

to the lightful full—

    Ah!!!

      why...look!

November 3, 2022

Postscript

now and then

where is now? where is then?

is now the now and also the then

and both are here in the everlasting circle

see how now and then blend, soak colors   soak lives
into each other

each moment of then creating now.

each moment of now creating then.

is this what we call minutes in now?

now emerges from then' s horizon

first peeping from the tree edges of earth-bodied now

the seeing, growing spreading to

the entire constant sky, the arc of now.

all who live in then

live in now

all who live in now live, too, in then

their voices speak our now

they speak now,

we speak now.

Do you believe this?

I do.

December 21, 2022

About the Author

Mary Ellen Weir has published her poetry in various journals and reviews. Her first book, *The Idea of More; The Question of Dust*, appeared in 2020. She holds a Ph.D. in English and has been a college professor for 35 years, with 29 of those years teaching literature and creative writing at Belmont Abbey College.

www.ingramcontent.com/pod-product-compliance
Lightning Source LLC
Chambersburg PA
CBHW020407130626
46549CB00006B/2466